The Night Season

Rebecca Lenkiewicz's first play, *Soho – a Tale of Table Dancers*, was performed by the RSC and won a Fringe First at the Edinburgh Festival in 2000. Subsequently the British Council took it on tour to Israel and it was the opening play at the Arcola Theatre in 2001.

REBECCA LENKIEWICZ

The Night Season

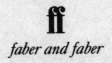

faber and faber

First published in 2004
by Faber and Faber Limited
3 Queen Square London WC1N 3AU

Typeset by Country Setting, Kingsdown, Kent CT14 8ES
Printed in England by Mackays of Chatham plc, Chatham, Kent

A CIP record for this book
is available from the British Library

ISBN 0–571–22475–X

2 4 6 8 10 9 7 5 3 1

For my family

Acknowledgements

I'd like to thank Howard Davies,
Nick Hytner, Dinah Wood,
Georgina Ruffhead, Jack Bradley,
Chris Campbell, Susannah Elliot-Knight,
Brigid Larmour, Ken Christiansen
of the Operating Theatre Company – and
finally Peter Quint for his permission to steal.

The Night Season was first performed in the Cottesloe auditorium of the National Theatre, London, on 23 July 2004. The cast was as follows:

Lily O'Hanlon Annette Crosbie
Maud Kennedy Sarah-Jane Drummey
Rose Kennedy Justine Mitchell
Judith Kennedy Susan Lynch
Patrick Kennedy David Bradley
John Eastman John Light
Gary Malone Lloyd Hutchinson

Director Lucy Bailey
Designer Dick Bird
Lighting Designer Neil Austin
Music Roddy Skeaping
Sound Designer Neil Alexander
Dialect Coach Majella Hurley
Movement Caroline Pope
Assistant Director Virginia Elgar

Characters

John Eastman
in his thirties

Patrick Kennedy
in his fifties

Judith Kennnedy
in her thirties

Rose Kennedy
in her twenties

Maud Kennedy
in her twenties

Lily O'Hanlon
in her seventies

Gary Malone
in his thirties

Patrick is father to Judith, Rose and Maud.
Lily is their maternal grandmother.

The action takes place in and around
the Kennedys' home near Sligo.

THE NIGHT SEASON

Act One

SCENE ONE

The kitchen. Late. Lily sits playing patience by lamplight. 'Just the Way You Look Tonight' is playing quietly on the record player. Lily is variously singing to it and reciting psalms to herself. She sings and hums the song on and off during the next scene.

Judith's room. There are two beds. Maud and Judith are in one, while Rose sits on the other near the window.

Rose She never goes to bed now.

Maud Will you miss her when she dies?

Rose No.

Maud I hope she dies in her sleep, though. Peaceful.

Rose What did the doctor say? (*She lights up a cigarette.*)

Judith A few months. I thought you'd given up.

Rose I have.

Judith Right. 'Night.

Rose 'Night.

Patrick's room, next to Judith's. Both have a window. Patrick is asleep in bed. He is having a nightmare.

Patrick You . . . You'll get blood on the carpet . . . Who took the carpet? . . . Just leave me my tongue . . . I have uses for that. (*He groans as though he is being stabbed.*)

Judith's room. Maud opens the window.

Maud He's having a nightmare.

3

Rose He is a fucking nightmare.

Patrick's room.

Patrick (*asleep*) Sit still . . . It won't hurt . . . I have to cut your hair. (*He bellows.*)

The kitchen. Lily has heard Patrick's groan.

Lily Esther? Esther? What's he doing to you? Esther?

Judith's room.

Judith She never stops talking about Mum now.

Maud Did you ring Mum today?

Judith I left her another message.

Maud Why doesn't she come back, then?

Rose She's not interested.

Judith We should get Lily over to London.

Maud She'd never get on a plane.

Judith What if Lily dies without seeing her?

Rose She won't. Go and see Mum if you want to. You don't need an excuse.

Judith Do you not want to see her?

Rose No. I don't like her . . . What? I didn't choose not to like her. This fella's not turning up now, is he? I'm going back to my room.

Judith You can't. His flight might be delayed. Anything could've happened.

Rose Why doesn't he stay with the others at the hotel?

Judith He wanted to stay somewhere real.

Rose Christ . . . somewhere real?

Maud Do you think this fella will look like Yeats?

Judith He'll have to, won't he? You have to be similar. Like Kirk Douglas as Van Gogh.

Rose Or Charlton Heston as Moses.

Maud Maybe one of us'll fall in love with him.

Judith Goodnight.

Maud No . . . I couldn't do that to Kevin.

Rose Kevin's a communist. He'd understand.

Maud Mm. We've not had sex in ages. He says it's world issues are crushing his masculinity.

Rose How long is ages?

Maud Two months. Don't say anything, will you? . . . I've never seen him fully naked, you know.

Rose What do you mean?

Maud He doesn't like me to see his body. He's always got a long shirt on or something.

Rose But when you have sex?

Maud It's always in the dark. It feels fine. He just won't let me see it. Should it worry me?

Judith No. 'Night.

Maud 'Night.

Rose No. Some people have sex through a hole in the sheet, don't they?

Maud Is that supposed to make me feel better?

Rose I just mean by their standards Kevin's very liberal, isn't he?

Maud I suppose.

Rose Plus his mother's a freak. She's the type would have breastfed him till he was seven. Maybe he's a woman. Maybe it's all strapped on.

Maud No. He's just shy.

Judith Where did you leave Lily's diet sheet?

Rose Oh . . .

Judith You filled it in, didn't you? I've got to give it to the doctor tomorrow.

Rose I'll do it before you go.

Judith Rose. You said you'd do it.

Rose So I forgot. So report me to Amnesiacs Anonymous. I'll do it in the morning.

Judith It's meant to be done at the time.

Rose I remember what she ate.

Judith You should write things down, Rose. Make a list of important things you've got to do.

Rose If there was ever anything important to do, I would.

> *Rose smokes while Judith and Maud go to sleep. Lily sings the sailor song from Korda's* Thief of Baghdad *and Rose echoes it to her just as the song is echoed in the film.*

> *Patrick's bedroom. Patrick wakes from sleep. He is drunk. He leans out of his window.*

Patrick Is that the singing fucking sailor?

> *Rose stops singing, Lily keeps singing quietly.*

Rose Yeah.

Patrick Does Sinbad happen to have a cigarette on her?

Rose Yeah.

6

Rose puts two cigarettes in her mouth, lights them both and gives one to Patrick.

Patrick That actor fella never came.

Rose No.

Patrick They said he'd be here Tuesday. I stayed in for him all day yesterday and today.

Rose But you never go out.

Patrick I stayed in.

Rose You've been asleep all day.

Patrick Yes. Staying in for him.

Rose Were you at the Pegasus tonight?

Patrick Tonight. Last night. Tomorrow night.

Rose Many people there?

Patrick Too many people. Do they have no homes to go to?

Rose Nikki behind the bar?

Patrick She was. Stood there under that blue light. The patron saint of the pissed. She haunts me. Those eyes, that dress, those breasts.

Rose Were the film people there?

Patrick Fucking circus. Gifford was showing off to the make-up girls. Doing the same old fucking light-bulb trick.

Rose Which one?

Patrick Smashing it in one hand while he drinks his pint with the other. I held the stool for Nikki while she changed the bulb. She had her jeans on tonight.

7

Rose 'Night, Dad.

Patrick That moon is fucking bright.

Rose Sweet dreams.

Patrick The devil takes care of his own.

They go to their beds.

SCENE TWO

The Pegasus. John Eastman sits down with a pint and a whiskey. He is very abstracted and quite drunk. He is wearing a dinner suit. Gary has also had a few drinks and approaches him.

Gary (*gives John a wallet, a script and a packet of cigarettes*) You left your stuff on the bar.

John Thanks.

Gary Are you all right?

John Yes. Thank you.

Gary Are you here with the film?

John Yes. You?

Gary No. I live here. Gary Malone.

John John.

Gary Are you an actor?

John Yes.

Gary Cigarette?

Gary offers John a cigarette. John tries to light it, but has difficulty because his hand is shaking. Gary lights his own and helps John to light his.

John Thanks. Can you help me, Gary? Later I need to get to this house. There's no phone number. Do you know where it is? Or where I can get a cab? (*He gives Gary his diary with the address written in it.*)

Gary No need . . . It's not far. I'll walk you there when you've finished your drink.

John I just need to know how to get there.

Gary Do you know the family?

John No. You do?

Gary Yeah, I do.

John What are you drinking?

Gary I've one at the bar (*to the barmaid*) I'm coming back for that, Nikki! (*to John*) Is that clothes she's wearing or underwear? (*to Nikki*) Get your thieving hands off that! You tell me when you want to go up to the cottage. No hurry.

John Did you ever do something irreparable, Gary?

Gary What?

John Something shameful you could never repair?

　Gary sits down.

Gary You can't tell, can you?

John Why not?

Gary You might fix things later.

John Sometimes you know.

Gary What did you do? Did you kill someone?

John Do you think you know when you love someone?

Gary Yes. I think it's pretty clear.

9

John And if you do, you can do anything, can't you? Love makes you brave.

Gary It can work the other way. Make you an awful coward.

John No. Not real love. It makes you fearless. That's why people crave it. They want to be transformed.

Gary Maybe. You left someone behind?

John Yes. I should have picked her up in my arms and I didn't.

Gary Talk to her.

John It's too late.

Gary I'm sorry.

John Thanks . . . Your face changed.

Gary My face?

John When I showed you that address. Your expression changed.

Gary They do change, don't they? Else it'd be pretty fucking boring wouldn't it?

John 'But one man loved the pilgrim soul in you and loved the sorrows of your changing face.'

Gary You been learning Yeats?

John There's a lot in the script.

Gary He's got some great chat-up lines.

John Something happened to you in that cottage.

Gary Not something. Someone.

John And you love her?

Gary She . . . affects me.

John And she doesn't want you?

Gary I haven't asked lately.

John Were you together?

Gary We were. A long time ago.

John And now you're apart.

Gary I'm here. She's there.

John And she didn't fight for you?

Gary No, she didn't.

John That's pretty conclusive, isn't it?

Gary I'm going to get my drink. I'll walk you there when you're through.

Gary goes to the bar. John drinks his whiskey.

SCENE THREE

The kitchen. Late. Lily is in her chair. Rose enters and sits by the fire.

Lily Esther?

Rose No, it's me. Do you want a cigarette?

Lily Absolutely. Is the rain keeping you awake?

Rose lights two cigarettes and gives one to Lily.

Rose No.

Lily Esther used to come down like that. As a child. In the middle of the night. There's a man outside sat waiting by the wall in the rain. He has no shoes.

Rose (*goes to the window*) No. There's no one there. Do you want a drink?

Lily Yes. Why were you crying last night?

Rose gets them both a drink.

Rose I just felt blue. Thinking that things might never happen.

Lily Young men?

Rose No.

Lily You were scared you'd be a spinster all your life.

Rose I'm not a spinster. I'm single.

Lily Is that different?

Rose Very different.

Lily But neither of them has a man. You were crying because you're a spinster.

Rose Do you want to go to London with Judith and see Esther?

Lily No. There's too many directions there.

Rose I'm going to bed. Do you want anything?

Lily A lover.

Rose exits. Lily stares into the fire.

Do you see the lion in the fire, Esther? Do you remember your huge lion? We'd visit him in the shop and talk to him. Then one day he disappeared and you mourned him. But he was next to your bed in the dark, waiting . . .

A gentle knock on the door. Lily goes to it and opens it to John, who is barefoot and drunk. He is holding his muddy shoes.

John Hello. I'm John. The light was still on.

Lily You have no shoes.

John No. I took them off.

Lily You're wet. I'm Lily.

John I'm staying next door. In your cottage. Do you stay up all night, Lily?

Lily I don't like to be horizontal. Whiskey?

John I'd love one.

Lily I saw you. Waiting. Like the song. (*She sings a couple of lines from 'Lili Marlene'.*) People said I was like her because of my name and my face.

John Who were you like?

Lily Lili Marlene. He was tired marching and he thought of her and his bags got lighter. Would you like to dance?

John Dance?

Lily With me.

John I would, but . . .

Lily You don't want to. I see that.

John No. I'd love to. Shall we?

He takes her hand and gently dances cheek-to-cheek with her. They hold each other tighter. Marlene Dietrich's 'Lili Marlene' plays.

Lily Do you hear the music?

John No. But I can imagine it.

Lily Do you dance with everyone?

John No. I don't.

Lily Nobody's paying you, are they? To dance with me?

John No, they're not.

Lily Nobody's behind that red curtain, are they? Watching? Laughing?

John No. Nobody's there.

Lily Your feet are naked. They're deeply personal. I don't remember the last time I was alone with a man. I don't remember what a man is like. I knew men in a past life. You're real, though, aren't you?

John I think so, Lily. I don't really know.

Lily There's too many details for it not to be happening. Our shadows are dancing together too. Authentic. You've a wonderful touch. I feel so beautiful I could die. John, would you stay with me tonight? Please. I'll clean your shoes for you in the morning.

John Course I'll stay with you. And I'll clean my own shoes.

> *They dance. Lily sits down on the floor. John puts a blanket over her and lies down to sleep. Lily sits and watches him. The music fades.*
>
> *Outside. Gary is standing in the rain, very drunk. He is looking up at Judith's window.*

Gary Judith? Do you want to come out for a walk? Judith . . . I played chess the other night against myself and each of the pieces looked like you. Even the bishops. I sit in my room and I wait for you. Thinking you might turn up on the doorstep in the rain. I'd make you tea and dry your hair. Fuck it. People ring the bell and it's not you. I'm going away. 'I have loved a queen beyond measure and exceeding long' . . . and now I'm tired. So fucking tired. And I'm going away.

SCENE FOUR

Morning. Lily is still watching John.

Lily You look like a child.

John (*waking*) Morning.

Lily Good morning, John. How are you?

John I'm fine. Bit of a headache.

Lily You fell off cliffs in the night and shouted. (*She puts a feather in his hair.*)

John Did I keep you awake?

Lily No. I don't sleep. Would you like some music? I've a surprise record for you, John. Can you guess what it is?

Judith's room. Judith, Rose and Maud are getting dressed and making their beds.

Rose Are these my tights? I can't live like this for six weeks. Like a fucking gypsy.

Maud How much'll we get, do you think?

Rose Nothing if Dad gets it first.

Judith Don't let Kevin get his hands on it either.

Maud What do you mean?

Judith Don't let him beg it off you.

Maud He wouldn't. He's not like that.

Rose He asks you for his bus fare home.

Maud He only asked me for it once.

Judith Twice. And he asked me to delete his library fines.

Maud Which you didn't do. Which I ended up paying.

Judith Which I gave back to you. He was arrogant. He said the silence signs were forms of government censorship. Plus I see him nicking books.

Maud It's not a crime to lend him money, is it?

Judith Does he give it back to you?

Maud He means to.

Judith I'm not attacking you. I'm just saying that when Dad gives you that money –

Rose If Dad gives you that money –

Judith Go and buy yourself something nice. Don't give it to your man.

Rose Do you think Kevin's actually terrified by his own genitalia?

Maud I don't know why I ever tell you things.

Judith I'm late. Will you two get Lily breakfast?

Rose No. We'll ritually starve her and record her reactions in her diet journal.

Judith, Rose and Maud exit the bedroom.

The kitchen. Lily and John are sitting up on the floor with a blanket over them. They have tea, toast and cigarettes. Marlene Dietrich's 'Johnny' is playing.

Lily Shall we listen to it again?

John Three times was fine, thank you. Just perfect.

Lily Would you like some more tea? Toast? Cigarettes? Whiskey? Cheese? Eggs? Tea? Toast? Jam?

John Nothing. Thanks.

Judith, Rose and Maud enter.

16

Judith Lily . . .

Lily Yes . . . This is Judith, Rose and Maud. This is John.

John Morning.

Judith You're John Eastman?

John I am. I got here very late last night.

Lily John's a wonderful dancer.

Judith Good. John . . .

John Lily asked me to stay in here with her, so I did.

Judith Right. Are you all right, Lily?

Lily I'm fine, Judith. How are you?

Judith I'm well. Very well. I have to go to work. Shall I show you next door?

Maud I'll take him.

Judith I'll see you, then.

John Bye.

Judith Should I call Dad before I go?

Patrick enters with just a long shirt on.

Patrick I don't know why you have to play music in the morning, Lily. And why do you play the same fucking song over and over? You're not a fucking teenager. Who's got my fucking tobacco? Tea. Will somebody make some tea?

Maud Morning, Dad.

Patrick Where's my tobacco? Where the fuck is it?

Rose Have one of mine.

Patrick No, I want a decent smoke.

Patrick starts to deconstruct an armchair and to tear apart long-buried dog-ends to make a roll-up cigarette.

Lily That's what parasites do.

Patrick What?

Lily To the furniture.

John (*getting up now with his crumpled dinner suit minus jacket*) Hello. I'm John. How are you?

Patrick Dead, to all intents and purposes. Dead. I suffer from bad dreams. Excuse my *déshabillé*. You're not homosexual, are you?

John No.

Patrick Then it shouldn't bother you. Were you just in bed with Lily? I'm not passing judgement. She's over the age of consent.

Lily I was frightened. John stayed with me.

Patrick Good. There is too little kindness in the world . . .

Patrick is tearing more dog-ends apart.

Maud Dad. Don't do that. Have one of Rose's. Dad!

Patrick Terrible thing to embarrass your own children. Do you mind if I smoke dog-ends, John?

John No. But there's some fresh tobacco in my jacket pocket there if you'd like it.

Patrick Thank you. Would you like a drink? (*He pours out whiskeys for himself and John and gives him a drink.*) I find the first is the sweetest before fluoride or domestic worries have set in. While the ghost of your body is still a warm imprint on your sheets.

John Thank you.

Patrick takes out John's tobacco and starts making a roll-up. Looking for a light, he pulls out a large bag of weed.

Patrick What's this?

John It helps me to relax. Would you like some?

Patrick No, no, you're all right. I might try a bit sometime.

John Take it. Please. I've loads more. It's very nice. Strong.

Patrick (*looking at it and sniffing it*) That's very kind of you. The last time I possessed something like this was thirty years ago in Denver. Searching for Kerouac. I wanted to see the midget auto-racers. I didn't know if it was the cars that were midget or the people who drove them. Godforsaken place, Denver. A man stared out of a window and he was wanking – well, each to his own, but it was not such stuff as dreams are made on. What are you doing, Lily?

Lily (*taking out shoe polish and cloths*) I'm going to clean John's shoes.

John I'll do that.

Patrick Put the fucking shoes down. We were worried about you, John.

John Why?

Patrick We expected you to become one of the family on Tuesday.

John I couldn't leave London until yesterday. Did you not get the message?

Patrick No message arrived. People will steal anything these days. I walked into a café the other day to use the telephone. Never mind what for, I mean it was to make a call, but never mind who to. And sellotaped to the wall above the directories was a notice in biro. It said: 'No talking to imaginary strangers.' That's what the sign said. Because we are the loneliest and nearest to hell that we have ever been. Yet the western world smells so sanitised. It should smell like Golgotha. It should stink of rotting human flesh and pus and shit. But instead it smells like a McDonald's toilet. Do you ever frequent those hell-holes, John?

John I don't.

Patrick Good. I only ever enter them to defecate. My personalised gift to their corporation. Their cubicles have a consistent smell. That of a child's perfume and burnt skin. You can imagine the most terrible abominations going on in those red-and-yellow shitehouses. Have you eaten? Judith could make you a sandwich.

John I'm fine, thanks.

Judith I've got to go. See you all later.

Patrick I agree. Eating is a waste of time.

Maud See you.

John Goodbye.

Lily Will you see Esther?

Patrick Fuck's sake. She's in London, Lily. She's been there fifteen years. Remember?

Lily I do remember. I just forget.

Patrick Well, stop forgetting.

Judith See you. (*Judith exits.*)

Patrick Why did you ask to stay here, John, and not in a hotel?

John I wanted to stay somewhere quiet.

Patrick Do you not think that quiet is a state of mind?

Lily People die in hotels.

John They do. I should go and look at my script.

Patrick One of the girls will show you the cottage.

Maud We're not prostitutes, Patrick.

Patrick I asked you to show him the cottage, not fuck him. Sharper than a serpent's tooth. Do you know where that is from, John?

John *King Lear.*

Patrick He had three daughters too, didn't he? I feel for him. No wonder he went fucking mad. And that was without the mother-in-law. Will somebody show John his bed?

Rose Will you come with me, John?

John Thank you for the dance, Lily.

Patrick You have no bag? No trappings?

John They're at the pub.

Rose and John leave to go next door to the cottage, which adjoins the kitchen.

Lily It's better than a hotel because hotels have upside-down glasses in the bathroom to scare you.

Patrick What the fuck is scary about an upside-down glass?

Lily Because you can imagine yourself inside is why. Tiny and scratching at the sides and no one hearing you.

Rose's room. Rose and John enter.

Rose There's nothing to show, really. Bed. Window. Floor. Do you need anything?

John No. This is perfect.

Rose Towels are in the cupboard.

John Thanks. Is this your room?

Rose Yeah.

John So where will you stay?

Rose Upstairs. It's nice, all of us sharing for a bit. Shall I get you some tea or something?

John No. Thank you.

Rose I'll put the fire on. (*She switches on an electric fire.*)

John Thanks. (*He gets out a hip-flask and has a swig of vodka.*) Would you like some? Russia's finest?

Rose Thanks. (*He pours her a little into a glass on the bedside table.*) That's strong.

John It's the real thing. From Moscow.

Rose Were you there?

John I did a film there about the poet Esenin.

Rose Do you always play writers?

John And criminals. What do you do?

Rose I work at a bookie's . . . temporarily. I've a couple of weeks off while it's being refurbished. But I've got to find a different job.

John You don't like it?

Rose I hate it. Plus it's dangerous. There's been two hold-ups in the last three years.

John In such a small town?

Rose People pass through. Was Lily okay with you last night?

John She was great.

Rose It was good of you to be with her. I didn't realise she was frightened.

John I don't think she was. She just wanted a bit of company. Do you mind if I smoke in here?

Rose No.

John Thank you.

He offers Rose a cigarette, which she accepts.

Rose Thanks. (*She passes him a religious-looking ashtray.*)

John You went to Lourdes?

Rose Lily's sister Kitty. She used to go there every year. Did you see her in the front room?

John No.

Rose She's on the mantelpiece. Her ashes. So do you know your lines?

John Most of them.

Rose You're playing Yeats?

John I am.

Rose That's a nice part to play. (*Pause.*) Isn't it?

John It is.

Rose I'll leave you to it. Are you tired?

John Exhausted.

Rose You've cut your hand. It looks quite deep.

John Yes . . . I don't know how I did that.

Rose Do you want a plaster?

John No. It's fine.

Rose I'll get you one. There's some in the bathroom.

Rose goes into the adjoining bathroom.

John (*to Rose in the bathroom*) Thank you. I like your room.

Rose (*from the bathroom*) It's all right. It's nice in the morning . . . gets the sun. All the cats congregate on the roof out there.

She returns with a wet towel, TCP, cotton wool and a plaster and places them next to John.

You should clean your cut.

John I should.

Rose Are you filming tomorrow?

John Yes . . . unless it rains.

Rose Are you all right?

John Yes.

Rose We're in if you need anything.

John Is there a clock in here?

Rose No. I'll get you one.

John I forgot to pack one. My mother died.

Rose Your mother?

John Yes. On Tuesday.

Rose God. I'm sorry. Had she been ill?

John Yes. She was very ill. Very ill.

Rose And they expect you to work still?

John They shifted scenes round me for a couple of days. So I could stay for the funeral.

Rose I'm sorry.

John No. I'm sorry. I'm not quite sure where I am or what I'm doing.

Rose Course you're not. Give me your hand. (*She cleans his cut, puts a plaster on it and holds his hand.*)

John Thank you.

Rose You should be with your family.

John No. Probably best to work.

Rose Get some sleep.

John Yes, I will. Sorry.

Rose Don't be sorry.

She takes her hand away and John curls up on the bed. Rose takes a blanket from the cupboard and puts it on him.

Are you warm enough? Shall I get you more blankets?

John No thank you.

Rose Shall I draw the curtains?

John Yes, please.

Rose Are you all right on your own?

John I think so. I don't really know.

Rose Shall I stay with you a while?

John Yes. Please.

Rose sits on the bed and takes his hand.

Thank you.

She curls up next to him.

Thank you . . . ?

Rose Rose.

John Rose.

They lie together.

SCENE FIVE

The Library, the same morning. Judith is sorting through a pile of books. Gary walks in and bangs down a pile of books.

Gary This is a hold-up. Give me all your Dostoevskys.

Judith Hi, Gary. Do any of these want renewing?

Gary I don't believe in it. I had a drink with your actor fella.

Gary handles the books on the desk. One is large with a mirror-type cover that reflects one's face.

Is this a book or a mirror?

Judith Self-help.

Gary I don't think it would help me. Staring into that. (*handling several Yeats books*) You reading Yeats?

Judith I thought that John might be interested in them.

Gary Do you remember when we did Yeats at school? Everyone laughed because Miss Cooper read from his diaries about him being celibate for seven years? (*reading*

26

from one of the books) 'Half-close your eyelids, loosen your hair.' Do you think she did?

Judith You look tired.

Gary You look beautiful. You didn't hear or see me last night, did you?

Judith No. Are you in trouble? What have you done?

Gary Nothing. Only I walked John up to yours after the pub chucked us out. You were sat in the dark by your window. I watched you. I was going to climb up to you but I thought you'd laugh. And the wall was very wet.

Judith You tried to climb up?

Gary For a moment. I was drunk. Then I just looked up at you.

Judith What did I look like?

Gary Very beautiful. Sad. Incredibly young.

Judith I wouldn't have laughed at you.

Gary No?

Judith No. I was asleep. It was Rose you were staring at.

Gary Rose?

Judith She's staying in my room while John's here.

Gary I assumed it was you . . . (*He starts to walk out.*)

Judith Gary . . .

Gary What? What is it, Judith Kennedy? What do you want?

Judith What? It's not my fault you were chatting up my sister. I wanted to ask you something. Are you busy next Friday?

Gary I'm going away next week.

Judith Where to?

Gary London. To live. What do you think?

Judith I think that's great.

Gary Do you?

Judith I do.

Gary What did you want to ask me?

Judith Nothing. What'll you do there?

Gary I've a few games lined up.

Judith Where will you stay?

Gary There's a room come up at Liam's. Will you come and see me over there?

Judith Maybe. Will you send me a postcard?

Gary Never liked them. They always seemed a bit public. See you.

Judith Will you bring all your books back tomorrow?

Gary Possibly . . . Can I not keep them as past services rendered to the library?

Gary exits and Judith sits down.

SCENE SIX

Rose's room. Rose and John are in bed naked. Rose pulls the sheets over her.

John Are you all right?

Rose Yes. You?

28

John Yeah. (*He reaches over to his cigarettes and lights one. He offers one to Rose.*)

Rose Thanks.

  Pause.

John Getting dark outside.

Rose Yeah.

John The days are very short.

Rose Yeah.

John The sound of the rain is nice.

Rose It is.

John Do you have to go?

Rose No. Do you want me to go?

John No.

Rose Can I ask you something?

John Anything.

  Pause.

Rose Did you love your mother?

John Yes. I think so.

Rose Did you see her when she was dead?

John Yes. Twice. First at the hospital.

Rose What was that like?

John Horrible. I wanted to lift her out of the bed and carry her home through the park.

Rose But you didn't?

John No. No, I didn't. Then I saw her in the Chapel of Rest.

Rose How was that?

John Grim. She looked like a man who had put on too much blue eye-shadow. Terrible smell. Like the labs at my old school.

Rose Did you feel angry?

John No. I wanted sex. I wanted to find someone on the street and fuck them. I got porn videos out and spent the night watching them. Wanking. One was set in a hospital. Am I going to hell?

Rose No. If I saw my mother dead I'd feel absolutely indifferent. Am I going to hell?

John No.

Rose gets up and finds various garments and shoes around and in the bed. She starts to get dressed.

John You've got a beautiful body.

Rose Have I?

John You have.

Rose You're my first lover, John.

John I'm not?

Rose Course you're not. I just thought it sounded nice. I like your nose.

John My nose?

Rose Your eyes and everything too. But you seem to think with your nose.

John Makes me sound a bit like a spaniel.

Rose You are a bit like a spaniel. They're nice.

John Not particularly heroic though, are they?

Rose They are. They go splashing into ponds without thinking and they race around after sticks.

John Is that your idea of heroic, Rose?

Rose They're fearless.

John And a bit stupid.

Rose No they're not. I like your jawline too. I like the way it curves here . . . (*touching his jaw*) Are you still aching? For more sex?

John It's . . . a pretty strong ache.

She puts her hand under the sheet, touches him.

Rose Is that making it any better?

John That's helping. That's helping a lot.

Rose continues . . .

Rose There?

John Yes. Just there.

Rose So you don't like spaniels?

John I think they're . . . fantastic.

Rose But stupid.

John No. I think they're phenomenally intelligent. Hugely . . . hugely cerebral creatures . . . oh yes . . . very very . . . very . . . yes . . . yes.

Rose kisses John and starts to take her clothes off.

The kitchen. Maud, Patrick and Lily are watching the TV.

Maud Can we put the sound up?

Lily It's my house and it's my turn and I like the sound down.

Patrick It's no use trying to reason with a lunatic.

Lily I'm not lunatic. I'm selective. I'm going to ask John to come to the beach with me tomorrow. Do you think he'll come?

Patrick He's here to make a film not fucking sandcastles.

Judith comes in from outside.

Judith Hiya. John not here?

Lily He's taking me to the beach tomorrow.

Judith What's this? (*She sits down to watch it with them.*)

Maud Robert Mitchum. Speechless.

Lily John's taking me to the beach tomorrow. He promised.

Patrick You haven't even fucking asked him yet.

Judith Who's taking you?

Patrick I'm not.

Maud I can't. I've got to revise.

Rose enters from outside.

Lily Rose will take me. You'll take me, won't you, Rose?

Rose Take you where?

Maud Where did you go?

Rose Into town.

Lily To the beach. With John. Tomorrow.

Maud What did you go into town for?

Rose I needed to buy something. I think he'll be working, Lily.

Maud So where is it?

Rose What? Oh, they didn't have it.

Lily Why have you no coat? You'll become an Inuit.

Rose What are you watching?

Patrick Fuck knows.

Rose Why are you up, Dad?

Patrick My room smelt of earth. I thought I'd take John down the Pegasus. Introduce him to Gifford and the boys. Is someone making tea? Judith?

Judith gets up to make the tea.

Lily Will you take me, Rose?

Rose Yeah, we'll get the bus. Just the two of us.

Maud He doesn't look like Yeats. He's much better-looking. Don't tell him I said that. Is he married, do you think?

Lily He doesn't smell married to me.

Maud What does a married man smell like?

Lily Like rubber. And their necks are thicker than John's.

Maud Did Grandad smell like rubber?

Patrick He smelt like Jamesons.

Lily The bastard stank of rubber.

There is a knock on the door. John enters.

Patrick No need to knock, John. Not unless it's for dramatic effect. Will you eat with us?

John I don't want to put you to any trouble.

Patrick You're not. I never cook. The girls are dying to know if you're married.

Maud We are not. Nobody said that.

Patrick Are you beholden to somebody back at the OK Corral? Are they waiting to see you ride back through the sunset? Maud thinks you're much better-looking than Yeats. Which is not a great feat. He had a very weak chin, didn't he? He should have grown a beard.

John What are you watching? Robert Mitchum?

Patrick *Night of the Hunter* . . . the silent version.

John Is there something wrong with the telly?

Patrick No. With Lily.

Lily Would you like the sound up, John?

She goes to the television and turns the sound up. The dialogue on screen is about love and hate.

Maud Rose, you've been all around town with your jumper on inside out.

Rose Who wants a drink?

Maud You, I should think.

Rose gets a bottle of whiskey out and downs a glass.

Rose Dad? John?

Lily What about me?

34

Rose Would you like one?

Lily No.

Patrick (*indicating the television*) You must stay and eat, John, else you'll never know if good prevailed over evil. Now that you're one of the family you must be a part of our rituals. Then you can come on down to the pub. Meet Gifford.

Maud Don't say yes if he asks you for an arm-wrestle.

Patrick And I'll introduce you to an angel with the biggest . . .

Judith Stay. Eat.

John I will if that's not a problem.

Patrick There are no problems in this house. Only disasters. Goodbye, progeny. I'll see you in a bit, John.

John See you there.

Judith 'Bye, Patrick.

Maud 'Bye, Dad. Spy on Kevin for me if he's there.

Patrick Goodnight, Lily. Remember me at my best.

Lily (*quietly*) Fuck off.

Rose 'Bye, Dad . . .

Judith I brought you some books about Yeats. I work at the library. You might have them already. But there's lots of pictures. (*She hands John the books.*)

John That's very thoughtful. Very kind. I've not seen these before.

Lily If we're going to have the sound up then we're not allowed to talk. Except for John. And except for me. Or if someone catches on fire.

They sit and watch the film silently for a few moments.

John?

John Yes.

Lily Do you have plans for tomorrow?

John We're filming. Unless it rains.

Lily What time are the buses, Rose?

They sit as more dialogue about love comes over the screen.

SCENE EIGHT

Rose and John are on the beach. It is raining. Lily is having a pee nearby, out of sight.

Lily (*shouting, from out of sight*) Rose! It's coming out of me like a horse!

Rose (*to Lily*) Great. You let me know when you're finished.

Lily (*out of sight*) It's like the yellow rivers of Babylon . . .

Rose Shall I come over?

Lily I want no help.

Rose I'm sorry if Lily was insistent about today.

John She wasn't. She just said that I'd promised to come here with her and that she was probably going to die very soon.

Rose I'm sorry.

John Don't be. It's great here.

Lily (*out of sight*) Do you want to pee now, Rose?

Rose (*to Lily*) No.

John You were very wild and kind yesterday.

Rose You were very fucking sexy. Subject closed.

Lily (*approaching*) Which subject? Were you watching the birds?

John Yes. They're wonderful.

Lily Shall we come here again tomorrow?

Rose We can't.

Lily I might come on my own. I'm going to collect some shells. Shall we make a fire?

Rose I think the wood might be too damp.

Lily I'm a bit scared.

Rose Of what?

Lily That you won't let me come here on my own tomorrow. Rose, I'm scared.

Rose What are you scared of?

Lily (*upset*) I'm scared that John thinks I'm stupid. I'm scared that you two want to be alone together and that you'll go away and leave me here. And I'll become the size of a pebble and someone will step on me.

Rose Give me your hand.

Lily What if you're asking for my hand and you want to hold John's? You hold Rose's other hand, John . . . Those birds sound like they're hurting. Everything sounds like it's in pain. Forgive me.

Rose For what?

Lily Anything. Please.

Rose Of course.

Lily I have told lies.

Rose We all tell lies.

Lily Am I ill?

Rose Do you feel ill?

Lily One minute I'm full and the next minute I'm empty. I'm freezing. Is it cold or is it me?

John It is cold. Would you like a coffee? Tea?

Lily Yes, please. Coffee, please. White. Two sugars. Can I have a cake too? From the sad man in the van?

John Of course. Do you want a coffee, Rose?

Rose I'd love one. Thanks.

    John goes off to get some coffees.

Lily I should go away and leave you both. I'll go for a walk with my cake. My legs are like those maps we felt at school. Why are you sad?

Rose I'm not.

Lily Scared?

Rose No.

Lily Of John?

Rose No. Why do you say that?

Lily Your hands are trapped.

Rose Really?

Lily Yes. You want to hold his hand?

Rose I don't know what I want.

Lily You want a paradise on earth and you don't want to live in paradise alone.

Rose Yes.

Lily I lied to your mother. When she was little. I told her that everything was going to be like a fairy tale. I said that she would go to parties all the time. She's not dead, is she? My Esther?

Rose No. She's not dead, Nan.

Lily No. Me neither. Do you want to fuck John?

Rose Shut up, Lily.

Lily The question is a fair one.

Rose Be quiet.

Lily Don't address me as though I were a child. I have had men inside me. And children. Don't put me in a cot.

John comes back with the coffees.

You bought everything, John. Don't the cakes and crisps look nice together? I'm going to collect some shells and find some feathers. Don't drink my coffee. Or touch my Wagon Wheel.

Lily leaves Rose and John. She sings the sailor song from Thief of Baghdad *as she walks away*

John She looks about ten years old.

Rose She says she wakes up and feels a different age every day. That the concept of time means nothing to her now so she has no fear of death. Have you spoken to your family today?

John No. I haven't. I've just been going over the script.

Rose Is it good?

John Terrible.

Rose So who's playing Maud Gonne?

John Anjelica Ryan?

Rose Is she Irish?

John Californian.

Rose Do you know her?

John No. Apparently she's a bit neurotic. Her agent has written a thesis on what she can and can't show in the sex scenes.

Rose I thought those two never had sex.

John They do in this film. Frequently. Always near swans.

Lily approaches humming 'Isn't this a lovely day to be caught in the rain?'

Lily Where's my Wagon Wheel? It's raining onto the sea. The patterns are terribly pretty. I have no womb, John. They took it out. How long will you stay with us?

John Six weeks.

Lily I'll be sad when you leave. I know a poem. 'I was a child and she was a child in our kingdom by the sea.' We learnt that at school. He loved her and she died. Do me a poem, John. From your film.

John What sort of poem?

Lily Anything as long as it's short. I'll close my eyes and imagine it.

John
    A mermaid found a swimming lad,
    Picked him for her own,
    Pressed her body to his body,

Laughed; and plunging down
Forgot in cruel happiness
That even lovers drown.

Lily Is it finished? I called Esther a mermaid because
we made her on the beach. Let's have a dance. I used to
win competitions with my sister Kitty. My husband used
to share me and Kitty on the dance floor, John. And
sometimes in the bedroom too. You two dance and I'll do
the music.

Rose I'm fine, Lily. You dance.

Lily Dance with me, John.

*They start to dance. Lily starts to hum 'Isn't this a
lovely day?' and sings it, and Fred Astaire's version of
'Isn't this a lovely day?' joins in.*

Come and dance with us.

Rose You're all right. I like watching you two.

Lily What do you think we are? Performing fucking
monkeys? Get off your ass, you miserable fucking spinster.
Get up and fucking dance with us.

They all dance together.

SCENE NINE

*The Pegasus. Patrick is finishing a pint. Judith approaches
him.*

Patrick What are you doing here?

Judith I live up the road.

Patrick Are you pregnant?

Judith No. Do you want another drink?

Patrick Jamesons. You sit. I'll go to the bar. What are you having?

Judith No, you're fine. I'll get them.

Patrick Don't deprive me of my vigil.

Judith (*looking to the bar at Nikki*) Oh, right. Is that a bikini she's got on?

Patrick It's a halterneck top.

Judith You're very well informed.

Patrick I asked her the same question earlier. What's Gifford doing sniffing round the bar?

Judith What's he done to his hand?

Patrick Tried to catch the moon. What'll you have?

Pause.

It's not a difficult question.

Pause.

Judith I've been thinking I might go and see Mum.

Pause.

Patrick Good.

Judith I might go on Friday. For a week. What do you think?

Patrick Have you bought your ticket?

Judith I have, yeah.

Patrick Then why ask me my opinion?

Judith Do you mind?

Patrick Why would I mind?

Rose Do you think I should?

42

Patrick Are you asking me if she'll be pleased to see you?

Judith Maybe.

Patrick Since when did I become the fucking oracle?

Judith You don't think I should go.

Patrick I don't think people should get up in the mornings. I don't think people should be allowed to talk to each other. Let alone affect each others' lives or decisions. I think people should live in isolation wards, not streets. (*He starts to move towards the bar.*)

Judith Shall I still stay for a drink?

Patrick Do as you will. You're not a child.

Patrick goes to the bar. Judith sits.

SCENE TEN

The kitchen. Rose is sitting near the fire, drinking wine. Late. There is a knock on the door. John enters.

Rose You don't have to knock. How was your dinner?

John Usual rubbish. Mostly about Anjelica and therapy and her new-found relationship with Maud.

Rose Is the director nice?

John Very nice.

Rose You finished late?

John Yeah. Can I sit down for a minute?

Rose Course you can. Do you want some wine?

John sits and takes off his scarf. Maud walks in, drunk, from outside.

Maud Has Kevin been here?

Rose No. I thought you were both at the Pegasus.

Maud We were . . . Oh shit.

Rose What is it?

Maud I thought he'd be here . . . I threw my pint over him.

Rose Why?

Maud Oh fuck.

Rose What?

Maud He says to me, 'Relationships change, don't they?'

Rose Yeah?

Maud Yeah. First they're great, then they're shit.

Rose You said that to him?

Maud No. But I kept asking him why he was distracted. He says, 'Oh it's politics,' and I know he's staring at Nikki's tits across the bar . . . then he has a go at me for getting a round in for everyone.

Rose Why?

Maud We're meant to be saving for Moscow. To visit descendants of Bakunin.

Rose Right.

Maud I've got to find him. I want to explode and there's no point unless he's there to hear it. Make him stay here if he comes. Will you?

Rose I will.

Maud exits.

Have you met Kevin?

John Yes. He talked to me about the film industry and explained to me how and why I was a prostitute.

Rose Will you have some wine?

Lily walks in.

Lily Who came home?

Rose Maud. Are you all right, Lily?

Lily (*upset*) I dreamt I had a baby but I forgot to feed it and its stomach became like a drum then I found it on a table and it was dead. I want to speak to Esther.

Rose The phone broke. Do you remember?

Lily I do. Patrick smashed it because Judith kept trying to ring London.

John Phone her on my mobile. I'll get it.

Lily Can I? 0044-208-493-6850. Thank you, John. Can I ring her from your room?

John Course you can.

Lily Will you take my hand?

Lily and John exit holding hands. Rose goes to the window and watches them go next door. She takes John's scarf from the back of his chair, smells it and puts it around her. She sits by the fire with her wine.

SCENE ELEVEN

The Pegasus. Judith and Patrick have had a few drinks together.

Judith Are you still angry with her?

Patrick No. No, I'm not.

Judith Do you still hate her?

Patrick I never hated her. I cut up her dresses but I never hated her.

Judith I thought you did.

Patrick It was a strange time.

Judith You told me one night that you raped her.

Patrick When did I say that?

Judith About a year after she'd gone.

Patrick You didn't believe me, did you?

Judith No. Why did you say it?

Patrick There were many times when I found myself geographically placed on top of your mother and I knew that she didn't want me there. That's probably what I meant.

Judith Do you remember that row we had? You said I'd grow up to be a 'fucking schoolteacher'.

Patrick I wasn't far wrong, was I?

Judith That was a bastard thing to say to a fifteen-year-old.

Patrick I was a bastard. I am a bastard.

Judith I should get some Taytos for Lily.

Patrick I found it painful that we grew distant.

Judith We didn't grow distant.

Patrick Didn't we? When Esther left you became obsessed with keeping the place tidy. You'd watch me with my wine and cigarettes, waiting for my ash to fall.

Judith I didn't.

Patrick My heart was hewn in two and you were worried about a fucking wine stain.

Judith You were all over the place.

Patrick We used to know each other. We grew apart.

Judith We still know each other.

Patrick No . . . Damage happened way before your mother left.

Judith What damage?

Patrick When you were eleven years old. You changed. You stopped being a child and you changed.

Judith Of course I changed.

Patrick Your heart changed but you denied it.

Judith I didn't feel anything less. Just differently.

Patrick I didn't like differently.

Judith I didn't like drunk.

Patrick That was me. That is me. I drink. I'd be the most miserable boring fucking bastard on the planet if I didn't. I'd be like the Ancient fucking Mariner. I'd corner you and start telling you something. You'd escape and when you came back in I'd resume from exactly where I left off. I'd be a bigger bully than I am now. I was scared of you, Judith.

Judith Scared of me?

Patrick I'm sorry. I didn't want to be. I always felt like you were waiting for me to fuck up. You always wanted to be right and I was always the villain.

Judith That's not fair. Not fair, Dad. I just wanted you to tell me that things were okay. And that you liked me. That was all I wanted. You were a bully. You didn't hit

Mum. You didn't hit us. But everything was so black or white. We were on your side or we weren't. We hated the system or we didn't. And you were always pissed and threatening to kill yourself. You were scared of me?

Patrick I was a terrible fucking father.

Judith You weren't. It was a difficult time.

Patrick Am I a bully?

Judith No, you're not.

Patrick A tyrant, then?

Judith No.

Patrick I'm sorry.

Judith For what?

Patrick I'm just very sorry that I have not served you better.

Judith You've been brilliant.

Patrick Don't defend me, Judith. This is my apology. In response to your attack.

Judith It wasn't an attack.

Patrick It wasn't a fucking love song. It's good that you say these things. I wish you'd said them at the time.

Judith I wasn't strong enough at the time.

Patrick No. I'm sorry if I was a bully.

Judith You weren't . . .

Patrick I probably was. Forgive me. Please. Forgive me, for fuck's sake.

Judith All right. All right. I forgive you.

Patrick Did I just bully you into forgiving me?

Judith No. I forgave you of my own free will.

Patrick When you were born, Esther kept bursting into tears saying she was scared she'd have to take you back. The yard was a paradise. Summertime. She'd sing to you. I'd roll her a cigarette and we'd all just lie there on a blanket. And I'd watch the smoke curling up from my hand and I thought, fuck, this is heaven. I'll get those drinks. Whiskey?

Judith I can't. I've got work tomorrow.

Patrick One more will do no harm.

Judith I'll have an orange.

Patrick Have a real drink. Judith, my child, my first-born. You've never been drunk, have you? In all your . . . how many years?

Judith Thirty, Dad. No I haven't. And I've no desire to. I'm going home.

Patrick Don't go. I'm sorry . . . I thought we might be gypsies for a night. Get slaughtered, plastered together. I'm sorry . . . I don't want another one either. I'll walk you home. (*He gets up.*)

Judith A pint of Guinness and a double whiskey, no ice.

Patrick Really? Shall we get drunk? You have to remember I'm a fool. I know not what I do sometimes.

Judith Am I meant to say that I'm a fool too now?

Patrick That would be a sort of drunken patois etiquette. I say something. You agree and emphasise it or you wildly disagree and we have an arm-wrestle.

Judith Okay, I'm a fool too. Sometimes.

Patrick You're the most beautiful fool I've ever seen.

Judith Thanks, Dad.

Patrick Have I upset you? You look sad.

Judith No. I thought you were getting the drinks.

Patrick I go. I go. See how I fucking go. Shakespeare, that is. Did you know that?

Judith I didn't.

Patrick See. I can still teach you things. I love you.

Judith Yeah. I know.

Patrick I'll get the drinks. (*He goes to the bar.*)

SCENE TWELVE

The kitchen. Late. Rose has drunk most of the bottle of wine. John enters.

Rose Did she get through?

John Yes. They're talking now.

Rose She's talking to Mum?

John Yes.

Rose Thanks for looking after Lily. Your drink's there.

John I'd better go to bed.

Rose Oh right. 'Night.

John 'Night.

Rose 'Night. Sweet dreams.

John Thanks . . . Rose . . .

Rose Yeah?

John Sleep well.

John exits. Rose stares into the fire.

Rose Do you see the dragon there, Mum? That long spark is his tail. And there's a woman. And a man there too. She's got her arms stretched out towards him . . . but I can't see what the man's doing. I can't see what he's doing.

> *We see John in his room. He walks in and goes to the bathroom to put water on his face. When he comes back into the bedroom he lights a cigarette. From the same jeans pocket that he takes his lighter, he takes a small piece of paper. He looks at it and burns it. Then puts his lighter back into this pocket. Then he lies on his bed and smokes. In the kitchen Rose switches on the record player. 'Night and Day' plays, it is scratched and jumps . . . Rose sits by the fire and listens . . .*

> *Like the beat beat beat of the tom tom*
> *When the jungle shadows fall . . .*
> *So a voice within me keeps repeating*
> *You . . . you . . . you . . . you . . . you . . . you . . .*
> *   you . . . you . . . you . . .*

SCENE THIRTEEN

Outside in a lane. Patrick is kneeling in a ditch, looking at the star-filled sky. Judith stands by him.

Judith You okay, Dad?

Patrick I'm just having a look.

Judith At the sky? Are you all right?

Patrick I am. Are you cold? Do you want my coat, 'cos it's fucking freezing out here.

Judith No no. You're all right.

Patrick starts to take his coat off.

Patrick I think you should wear this coat.

Judith No, you keep it on you. Are you getting up, Dad?

Patrick No. You see those fucking stars? Do you see them? Come here.

Judith I can see them from here. Are you getting up?

Patrick No. I'm in a position of worship. Come and kneel with me. Come on.

Judith Dad . . .

Patrick Don't worry about your tights. I'll buy you some new tights. Sit on my coat.

Judith No no. You're all right. (*Judith kneels down with him.*)

Patrick What do you think?

Judith Beautiful.

Patrick Better from down here, isn't it?

Judith It's beautiful.

Patrick Can you see the Great Bear? Can you?

Judith No.

Patrick No. Nor can I. Do you know what it looks like?

Judith No.

Patrick Me neither . . . those pictures of the constellations . . . they don't make sense . . . you get three stars in a triangle and a great big fucking eagle drawn around it with feathers and claws and a snake in its beak. Are you having a nice time?

Judith I am. I knocked a table over. Dad, I don't know if I can get up. Everything's spinning.

Patrick Just wait a moment. I'll get you up. Don't move.

Judith I won't. I can't. Thanks.

Patrick gets up and helps Judith to her feet. He takes her arm.

Patrick Can you walk all right?

Judith I don't know. I don't know anything. I'd like to see Gary. I really would.

Patrick Shall I take you to him?

Judith No . . . Could you, Dad? I don't know if I can walk.

Patrick Come here. You see? I can be useful.

He kneels down and gives her a piggy-back. He walks off with Judith on his back.

You tell me if you see any snakes.

'I Only Have Eyes For You' starts to play:

Are the stars out tonight?
I can't tell if it's cloudy or bright
'Cos I only have eyes for you, dear . . .

Interval.

Act Two

SCENE ONE

The kitchen. Later the same night. Rose is sitting drinking, while writing and listening to Marlene Dietrich's 'Lola'. There are screwed-up pages of a letter she is trying to write. Patrick crashes into something outside, glass smashes and he enters cursing, he has red on his hands and what looks like a black silk scarf around his neck. Rose abandons her letter and throws all the drafts into the fire. Patrick tries to fix himself a drink.

Rose Are you all right, Dad?

Patrick I need no assistance.

Rose Did you have a nice evening?

Patrick Nice is not a word I like to encourage.

Rose What have you done to your hand?

Patrick 'Blood. It will have blood.'

Rose Did you cut yourself?

Patrick No. Someone else.

Rose Have you been in a fight?

Patrick Since the day I was born.

Rose What happened, Dad?

Patrick There was no struggle. She came quietly.

Rose Dad . . .

Patrick Don't be scared, Rosie. I covered my tracks.

54

Rose Are you in trouble?

Patrick Very deep. Very dark. Are we alone? No, we're together . . . Groucho Marx . . .

Lily enters, abstracted.

Lily Did you bring Esther home with you?

Patrick No.

Lily Is she not here?

Patrick 'She wasn't here again today. Oh how I wish she'd go away.' Why did you name your daughter after a whore?

Lily What?

Patrick Esther. Ishtar. The whore of all whores.

Maud enters, sleepy and post-tearful.

Maud Judith's not come home. (*seeing his hands*) What's that? You been out with Gifford?

Patrick No. I've been painting. The town. Red.

Lily What have you got around your neck?

Patrick A scarf.

Lily No it's not.

Patrick A noose.

Rose Shall I take you to your room, Dad?

Patrick Like you took John to his room?

Rose What?

Maud Come on, Dad.

Maud helps him to stand up.

Patrick I'm not a child. And I'm not blind. 'Why, what could she have done, being what she is? Was there another Troy for her to burn?'

They exit.

SCENE TWO

Gary's flat. 4 a.m. Judith is sleeping, still drunk and out of it. Gary comes in with some water for her. Judith suddenly wakes.

Judith Rose!

Gary Judith. It's me.

Judith Gary . . . Gary, I thought I was somewhere else.

Gary Where were you?

Judith In a cellar. With Rose.

Gary Do you want some water?

Judith Yeah. Why am I here?

Gary I kidnapped you. Patrick and you were in the pub and I threw you over my shoulder and brought you home with me.

Judith No you didn't.

Gary Drink . . . it'll make you feel better tomorrow.

Judith Gary, I'm wearing foreign clothes. Where are mine?

Gary I hid them as part of my hostage plan.

Judith Where are they?

Gary They need washing. I'll take them to the launderette.

Judith What did I do? How did I get here?

Gary Patrick brought you.

Judith I was in a ditch with Dad talking about bears . . .

Gary You're all right. You've been a bit sick.

Judith No? What time is it? Should I be at work?

Gary It's four in the morning. You were having a nightmare.

Judith I stabbed Rose. She was bleeding to death and I did nothing. And I was hoping she'd die. Else she'd tell people it was me who killed her.

Gary Nobody's dead. Just drunk.

Judith Thanks, Gary. You look different.

Gary Different?

Judith God, it was horrible. I stood there watching her bleed onto the concrete floor. She was looking at me and she was in such pain.

Gary Was just a dream. Try to get some sleep now.

Judith curls up to sleep. Gary puts the blankets straight around her. Then he sits at a table with his chess set and account books.

SCENE THREE

Patrick's room. He is sitting on his bed, drink and roll-up in hand. He lights a candle and places it on a chair. He takes the black slip from around his neck, puts it on a clothes hanger and hangs it from a shelf, then turns the light out, pours himself a drink and raises his glass to the slip. He sits opposite the slip, watches it, approaches it, touches it.

Patrick An angel was flying in the dark night and I smote her down. I stole her from her lifeline and I wrapped her around my neck and nobody knew where she began and where I endeth. I salute you, patron silken saint of lost souls. I was in the desert and you gave me drink. You slaked my thirst. I was wracked on the wheel in the heat and you sang your gypsy song and gave me water. You have confused me. So perhaps I'm still alive. Terrifying thought. (*He laughs.*) It's very funny. No it is. (*He pours himself another drink.*)

SCENE FOUR

Rose's room, 4 a.m. John is in bed. Rose comes into the room. She is very drunk. She sits on the floor and watches him. She sits on the bed. He wakes.

John Shit!

Rose Did I wake you?

John God. What are you doing? What time is it?

Rose It's very early. Or very late. I wanted to see you.

John Right.

Rose Should I go?

John No. No . . . I'm just . . .

Rose You don't want me to stay, do you?

John Rose . . .

Rose It just felt like the right thing to come and see you. I knew it was wrong too but I thought if the world was going to end tomorrow and it really could because everything is so fucked up . . . if it was going to end tomorrow I'd choose to lie with you tonight. I'm drunk. Do you mind?

John I don't mind. But . . .

Rose Do you think I'm a slut?

John No. Course not.

Rose I think you think I am.

John No. I really don't.

Rose I don't do that with people. Not much. It just felt right.

John It was right. Very right.

Rose But it's not right any more?

John It's complicated.

Rose Why?

John What happened was . . .

Rose . . . beautiful.

John It was.

Rose And pure. I mean we were very dirty but pure in our dirtiness.

John We were.

Rose Should I go? I don't want to. I will but I don't want to. Can I have a cigarette with you then I'll go?

John They're on the table.

Rose takes one from the pack on the bedside table.

Rose Do you have a light?

John (*indicating his jeans*) In my pocket.

Rose I know I shouldn't have come in. But we spend all our lives doing shoulds and shouldn'ts, don't we? I was going to say there was something I needed badly from my drawer, but I thought . . . I just think you're beautiful.

I thought that when I first saw you. On the floor with Lily in a blanket. Like a couple of Red Indians. Sat there. I could imagine you running after horses. Then we were here together . . . . you . . . inside me. I felt it, you know? Very deep. And on the beach I wanted to cry because you were so kind to Lily and when we all danced it was nice, wasn't it? Dancing on the sand in the rain?

John It was. It was wonderful.

Rose I'm sorry. I shouldn't be here. This is your room.

John No. This is your room.

Rose I give it to you. Like I gave myself to you. I'll go after I've had a cigarette. I don't want to stop you from your sleep. You're fucking beautiful, do you know that?

John You're beautiful too.

Rose No. Sometimes. I felt beautiful in bed with you. And when I got up and collected my clothes I knew you were watching me. My arse. My back. And I knew you liked it. I shouldn't be saying this, should I?

John I did like it. I thought you looked gorgeous. You are very beautiful, Rose.

Rose No. Do you think Judith and Maud are beautiful?

John Yes. I suppose so.

Rose You don't or you do?

John Yes, I do.

Rose Who's the most beautiful?

John That's a bit silly.

Rose It's nice, though, isn't it? Being silly together? It's nice talking like this. So who is the most beautiful?

John You can't measure it like that.

Rose They can now. In America. They have a machine. It tells you who is the prettiest and who is the ugliest.

John Very useful.

Rose Should I go? No . . . Why should I go? You've only a holy ashtray to talk to. Shall I take you to another beach? There's beautiful beaches round here.

John That would be lovely. Sometime.

Rose Sorry. I'm drunk and you're not. I was just sitting by the fire, though, and it was so nice just drinking . . . thinking . . . drinking. Do you have a light?

John Jeans pocket.

Rose Thank you. For the light . . . I saw a programme about the ballerina Anna Pavlova. Do you know her?

John I've heard of her.

Rose She died. And she was meant to be dancing that night. In Paris. And everyone was there. All the musicians and the audience and everyone. All waiting for her. And then they got told she'd died. And do you know what they did?

John What did they do?

Rose (*becoming weepy with drink and emotion*) They did the whole thing . . . the whole ballet right from the beginning to the end with all the musicians and the dancers and they just shone a light where she was meant to be. They just shone one light and it moved round where she was meant to be dancing. And everyone watched the light and they knew she wasn't there but she was, you know? And I thought it was the most beautiful way to die in the world. (*crying*)

John (*putting his arm around her*) It was. It was.

61

Rose Sorry. I'll go in a minute. I'm sorry. It's all been a bit intense, you know? Did you ever feel that you were waiting for something and when it happened you couldn't handle it? It was too immense, too strange, or I don't know what. Do you? Do you know?

Rose feels in John's jeans pocket. She finds a pack of condoms as well as his lighter.

I thought you said you didn't have any.

John I didn't.

Rose You bought some?

John Yes.

Rose Today?

John Yes.

Rose And one of them's gone already.

John Rose . . .

Rose With the Californian?

John No. Somebody else.

Rose One of my sisters?

John No . . . Rose . . . nobody you know. I'm sorry.

Rose No. No. Don't be.

John I've upset you.

Rose I was upset before you got here. Just your coming here made me realise how upset I was. Goodnight.

John Rose. Come here. I'm sorry.

Rose Nothing's ever quite how you think it.

John I'm sorry.

Rose It's funny how you can surprise yourself, isn't it? I understand being surprised by other people, but to surprise your own self it's pretty fucking stupid, isn't it?

John I don't know.

Rose I do. It's incredibly fucking stupid. 'Night.

Rose walks out.

SCENE FIVE

Patrick's room. Dawn. Patrick is singing to the slip.

Patrick
'Down by the salley gardens my love and I did meet:
She passed the salley gardens with little snow-white feet.
She bid me take love easy, as the leaves grow on the
    tree:
But I, being young and foolish, with her would not
    agree.

In a field by the river my love and I did stand,
And on my leaning shoulder she laid her snow-white
    hand.
She bid me take life easy, as the grass grows on the
    weirs;
But I was young and foolish, and now am full of tears.'

SCENE SIX

Gary's flat. 10 a.m. Gary is sitting with his chess set and book. Judith is in bed.

Judith Morning.

Gary Morning. Do you want a game of chess?

Judith No.

Gary There's a cup of tea next to you. Should still be hot.

Judith Thanks. What time is it?

Gary Ten. I rang your work, said you were sick.

Judith What did they say?

Gary They hope you get very well very soon.

Judith I can't remember anything about getting here.

Gary You don't remember us having sex?

Judith We didn't.

Gary I was fantastic.

Judith Silly. Did I just crash out?

Gary No. You were talking about your mum. Then you kept asking why your dad would be scared of you. You cried and went to sleep.

Judith I vomit, then I weep. I'm sorry. How did we all end up here anyway?

Gary You told Patrick you wanted to see me.

Judith I'm sorry. Is this your shirt?

Gary No. It belongs to the woman I had to chuck out when you arrived.

Judith Were you asleep?

Gary No.

Judith I feel as if I've been in a fight. Can I stay here today? Am I in your way?

Gary No. You sleep as long as you want.

Judith That tea was good . . . You've not slept, have you?

Gary I'll sleep later. (*He gets out a notebook. He puts on a pair of glasses.*)

Judith What are you writing?

Gary I'm working something out.

Judith Have you some games booked in London?

Gary A few.

Judith When did you start wearing glasses?

Gary I just wear them for chess. Stops me getting headaches. And when I do the books. (*He moves a chess piece and writes the move down.*)

Judith Is it important that you win against yourself?

Gary Very. It's all about sacrifice and combination.

Judith Is it?

Gary Yeah . . . You have to set up a mating net. What do you reckon? Queen's Gambit or Kalashnikov Sicilian?

Judith They both sound pretty dangerous.

He moves a piece.

Which did you go for?

Gary Mm? I don't know yet.

Judith Do you remember when I first came round here? All you had was a striped mug and a mattress.

Gary And a tape recorder.

Judith I couldn't decide whether you were a poet or a murderer.

Gary I was both.

Judith You spent all your money on new sheets for when I came to stay the night and they were the wrong size.

Gary I don't remember that.

Judith You did. Could I have some water, please?

Gary brings her a glass of water.

Are you tired? You must be tired.

Gary I don't need much sleep.

Judith Come in with me. Sleep next to me.

Gary No. You're all right.

Judith Please.

Gary You want me to sleep next to you?

Judith No. (*He moves another piece and writes it down.*) Shall I tell you what I want?

Judith sits up on the bed.

Gary Yes.

Judith I want you to take off your clothes.

Pause. He tentatively starts to take off his shirt.

No. I want you to take off your clothes that are on me.

He takes off Judith's shirt.

Now I want you to take off your clothes that are on you.

Gary starts to take his clothes off.

Now I want you to kiss me.

He takes her head in his hands, which causes a severe pain.

Sorry, without moving my head too much. I'm trying to seduce you.

Gary I was getting that picture, yes.

Judith What do you think?

Gary I might not be able to. I'm a bit nervous. Do you mind?

Judith No. I don't mind, Gary.

They hold each other.

Gary Judith. Judith. Judith . . .

Judith Are you all right?

Gary Yes.

Judith kisses him.

Judith We can just hold each other, you know?

Gary No no no . . . I'll give it a try.

They embrace.

SCENE SEVEN

The kitchen. Lily and Maud are filling in Lily's diet sheet.

Lily Can I have a cup of tea? I feel as dry as Egypt.

Maud We've got to finish this, Lily. Judith'll have a fit if we've not done it again. Where did Rose go, anyway? I'm meant to be revising.

Lily My tongue cleaveth to my jaws.

Maud (*writing in the book*) What did you have for lunch?

Lily Slugs. I don't give a fuck. I just want a cup of tea. Why do they harangue and harass me, anyway? I'm going to die. So fucking what?

Maud They need to know if you have any allergies.

Lily I do. I have an allergy to diet sheets. Chuck it in the fire.

Maud Don't! That's a week's worth of journal.

Lily What difference if I ate peas before I died? Fuck it!

Lily and Maud have a tussle and the book gets torn. Lily feeds some pages into the fire.

Maud Shit.

Lily I want sex. Not iron pills. Good hard sex.

Maud I'll make the tea.

Patrick enters from upstairs. He is dressed smartly and starts to polish his shoes.

Maud You going somewhere, Dad? You want a cup of tea?

Lily Why is there ladies' underwear strewn in my yard?

Maud Do you want me to do that for you, Da?

Lily There are foreign clothes-pegs in the yard, Patrick.

Maud I'll do that for you, Da.

Lily Why are you anointing your shoes? It's not my funeral yet. You're just trying to scare me. You implied that Rose was a slut last night. And you took Judith out. You shouldn't have favourites. Am I your favourite? I'm John's favourite. (*She feeds her diet-sheet papers into the fire.*) 'Thou hast kept me alive, that I should not go down to the pit . . . What profit is there in my blood, when I shall go down to the pit? Shall the dust praise thee?'

Patrick leaves the house. Lily runs to the window to watch him go.

SCENE EIGHT

Gary's flat. Gary and Judith are in bed.

Judith You didn't seem particularly nervous to me.

Gary No. The nerves went. I got distracted and forgot about them.

Judith Was I distracting?

Gary Very. Was I?

Judith You were. Are you all right?

Gary I am. Are you having a nice day off work?

Judith I am.

Gary Is this what librarians do on their day off, is it?

Judith It is. We . . . we do some research into the outside world and then we write it all up and put it in a file in the reference section.

Gary Is it a file on the top shelf?

Judith It is.

Gary So that would mean you have to climb the ladder to put it away?

Judith Stop it.

Gary The library was vandalised last night, you know.

Judith It wasn't?

Gary There's red paint all over the wall. It says, 'Make as much noise as you fucking like . . . please!'

Judith No?

Gary Yeah.

Judith Hooligans. Do you think it was Kevin?

Gary No. I know who it was.

Judith Who was it?

Gary It was you and your dad.

Judith No. You're teasing me.

Gary No, I'm not. He said he was liberating the silence.

Judith God. I've become a drunk, a criminal and a harlot all in one night.

Gary It looks grand.

Judith Oh, Gary . . .

Gary It needed a bit of colour. You know what I used to like best about the library?

Judith What?

Gary When you'd say 'Shh' . . . I found it so fucking sexy. I'd stay in the reference section for ages just to hear you say it.

Judith You didn't? I thought you were there a lot. You were always noisy.

Gary To make you say 'Shh'. You want a cup of tea?

Judith Would you have to get up to make it?

Gary I would, yeah. I'd like to have an invention under my bed but all I've got's the kettle across the way.

Judith I'd love one.

Gary You be saying your Hail Marys while I'm making it. You've got a lot of them to do after last night and today.

Judith Shush . . .

Gary Don't you be doing that to me, Sister Judith. You know what effect that has upon a poor lost sinner like myself.

Judith Shh . . .

Gary Once more for while I'm in the kitchen.

Judith Shh.

They kiss. Gary half-dresses.

Judith When was the last time a woman inhabited these sheets? What? Who was it?

Gary Nikki. A few months ago.

Judith And before that?

Gary Stop it.

Judith I'm just curious.

Gary Last summer. A girl who played chess.

Judith Did she beat you? At chess.

Gary We didn't play.

Judith You spent the night together here? A few nights?

Gary Yes.

Judith Do you want to know my carnal history of the last few years?

Gary No. I don't want to know. I really really don't want to know. Thanks anyway. I'll get your tea. Do you want some toast?

Judith No. I've had no lovers since we parted. You're the only man I've known.

Gary Is that why you left me? Because you wanted to know other men?

Judith No.

Gary Why then?

Judith I didn't think you saw me as I really was.

Gary How did you think I saw you?

Judith As a sort of nun figure. In pain.

Gary Especially when you were on the library ladder. How do you think I see you now?

Judith As a vandal and a whore.

Gary Are you here, Judith?

Judith What?

Gary Now.

Judith I don't know, Gary.

Gary gets fully dressed, puts his jacket on and takes his keys.

Gary I'm going to get a paper.

Judith Are you angry?

Gary No. I'm tired. I'm wild tired.

He exits. Judith lies down.

SCENE NINE

The kitchen. Lily and Maud are watching the TV.

Lily Judith will see Esther tomorrow.

Maud She will.

Lily She spent fifteen pounds on a bottle of wine. Fifteen pounds. Will Esther meet her off the plane?

Maud I don't think so.

Lily Does she want him to do that or is he forcing her?

Maud I don't know. I can't hear what they're saying.

Rose walks in, very shattered.

Lily Where have you been all day?

Rose I went to the beach.

Lily John's gone. He left you a letter on your pillow.

Maud Are you all right?

Rose Great. Is Dad asleep? (*Pours herself a whiskey.*)

Lily He went out.

Rose Out?

Judith walks in.

Lily I threw my diet book on the fire.

Judith Good. That's good. Hiya.

Maud Hi. Did you stay at Gary's?

Judith I did, yeah.

Maud How was it?

Judith It was nice.

Maud So are you back on?

Judith No. No, we're not.

Maud So you still going to London, then?

Judith Yeah. Course I am.

Maud So what happened?

Judith I'm going to take some tea up to Dad.

Lily He's not there. He went to a funeral. It wasn't mine.

Judith What?

Maud I don't see how you can do that to Gary.

Judith Do what?

Maud He's waited years for you to go back to him.

Judith He's not a child.

Lily He was a child once.

Judith He's moving to London next week, anyway.

Maud Only 'cause you haven't asked him to stay. How come you got drunk with Dad anyhow?

Judith We were talking about Mum.

Maud Right.

Lily You defiled the library.

Judith I've left the doctors' appointments in the drawer. And when the gas bill comes there's a blank cheque. Just fill in the amount. All right?

Maud What?

Judith Gas bill. Cheque. Fill it in. Yes?

Maud Fine.

Judith Have you a message for Mum?

Rose Tell her I'm a slut and she's a bitch.

Lily Tell her she forgot my birthday card.

Maud I've some things for her. I put them by your bed.

Judith Post Office book is in here too.

Lily I helped Maudy wrap them. Gold tissue paper.

Maud They're next to your bed.

Judith How many things? Are they heavy to carry?

Maud Gary's waited years for you.

Judith What?

Maud Then you get together then you fuck off again.

Judith Did I ask you for your opinion?

Maud Don't talk to me like a fucking schoolteacher.

Judith Don't call me a fucking schoolteacher. What's got into you?

Maud Nothing.

Judith Just because you and Kevin are having a hard time there's no need to take it out on the rest of the world.

Maud It's got fuck-all to do with me and Kevin. Why do you twist things like that?

Judith I don't twist things. (*aware of the noise they are making*) Is John next door?

Lily He's not here. Will you stop talking about John John John now and let me listen to this?

Maud How can you listen to it with the fucking sound down?

Lily It's my telly. You be quiet.

Maud Fucking lunatic!

Judith Don't talk to Lily like that.

Maud I'll talk to her how I want to.

Judith You will not.

Maud Or what? Don't you tell me what to fucking do.
You're not my mother. Nobody ever asked you to act like
our fucking mother.

Rose Maud!

Judith What's this all about, Maud?

Maud What? I asked you to take something to Mum.
I asked you nicely. You only have to put it in your bloody
bag and you ask me how fucking heavy it is!

Judith I didn't mean anything by it.

Maud Yes you did. You can be so fucking selfish
sometimes.

Rose Maud, stop it!

Maud I won't. Why are you defending her anyway?
You're always saying how crap she's been to Gary?

Rose I'm not.

Judith Maudy, what is it now? Just tell us what's going on.

Maud Nothing. Fucking nothing. Fuck off and see Mum!
Go! Just fucking go! And don't bother to take my fucking
crap presents with you.

*Patrick comes in from outside. Maud tries to control
herself.*

Patrick Who's pregnant? Rose?

Judith Nobody's pregnant.

Lily I'm not either.

Patrick Good. Let's have a drink to celebrate. (*He pours
out some whiskeys.*) What's up, Maudy? Did Lily turn
the sound down again?

Judith Maudy's fine.

Patrick I went to the shops. I bought you some tights, Judith. (*He gives her a pair of tights.*)

Judith Thanks, Dad.

Patrick I took them to the library but I couldn't see you through the window and I thought it might not be politic to call at Gary's.

Lily Where's my present?

Patrick Here. I got you stockings, Lily. (*He produces two more pairs of tights and a pair of stockings.*)

Lily Anything else?

Patrick I got you all three pairs each. Do you want them now or shall I keep them somewhere? The woman said she'd change them if they're wrong. (*He puts the bag of hosiery on the table.*)

Lily They're very nice. Do you have a fancy lady who advised you on them?

Patrick No. Why did you say that? What have you heard?

Lily I've heard nothing.

Patrick The woman in the shop helped. I'm going out on Tuesday night. Just so you know. I asked Nikki if she'd like to go out for dinner with me and so we're going to go and eat something. Together. There's postal orders here from that company for the cottage rent.

Judith Thanks, Dad.

Patrick I've split it into four. Myself and Lily are sharing a quarter. You've the rest between you.

Judith Great.

Patrick I'm going to have a bath. Does anyone mind?

Lily No. Do you know where it is?

Judith Thanks for the tights, Dad.

Patrick exits.

Rose He's sober. He hasn't had a single drink, has he?

Lily Give me my money. Let me look at it.

Maud (*in tears*) He went and bought tights for us. Everything hurts, you know?

Judith Maudy . . . Maudy . . . come here . . .

Maud Don't. Please. Just leave me alone.

Judith No. no. Listen to me. If you want to come tomorrow you just come with me. I buy another ticket and you come. It's easy.

Maud It's not easy. It's not fucking easy. She never asked me to come.

Judith She didn't ask me either.

Maud (*crying*) I want her to ask me. I don't want to gatecrash my own mother's flat. I want her to ask me how I am.

Judith (*crying*) I'm sorry, I was stupid. I'm so sorry. It's all right, Maudy. Sweetheart, it's all right.

Maud (*crying*) It's not all right. You all know her. You had more time with her. I never knew her. Not really. You say when Mum did this, when Mum did that, and I don't remember. I don't remember. Judith, I'm sorry. I'm so sorry.

Judith Maudy, it's fine, you cry, it's fine. (*taking her in her arms*)

Maud He went to the shops.

Judith (*holding her*) He did. He did. Will you come with me to London?

78

Maud No no. I don't want to go. Really really I don't. I'm just being stupid.

Lily Maudy. Look, Maudy. You've three hundred pounds.

Maud That's great, Lily.

Lily And I've a hundred and fifty.

Rose A date with Nikki? Fucking hell.

Maud Do you think he'll make a fool of himself?

Judith No. As long as he doesn't get too drunk.

Rose He wouldn't bring her back here, would he? I can't imagine Nikki's breasts in Dad's room.

Judith I bet he can.

Rose I bet he does.

Lily Little Nikki. I remember her running around the park naked with a bottle.

Rose Pretty much what she does now every Saturday night.

Maud What are you going to get with your money, Lily?

Lily Do you think I should save it?

Maud No. You're not allowed to. You have to spend it.

Lily Could I get . . . ? I don't know what to get. What can I get?

Maud What do you fancy? Music? Underwear? Chocolates?

Lily I'd like to buy some chocolates. But I would like to get something else too. Do I have to spend it all on one thing?

Maud No. You could get chocolates and then something else.

Lily An animal?

Maud You could get an animal but you'd have to tell us what it was.

Lily I'd like a snake, but I think it's cruel. I don't want anything in a cage. I might want a dress that's all blue and sparkling and some shoes the same and a bag and a necklace. Have I enough for that?

Judith I'm sure you do, but would you wear it, do you think?

Lily I would. Every day. Every single day. I'm going to buy you something with my money, Maud.

Maud No. I have my own. You spend it on yourself.

Lily I wanted to buy you the same dress I was going to get.

Maud No, Lily. You'd wear it better.

Lily Your mother used to sing to you when you were babies. Would you like to watch the television with the sound up?

Maud sits on the arm of Lily's chair. Lily turns the sound up.

SCENE TEN

The Pegasus. Gary and Patrick are having a pint together.

Patrick Gifford been in tonight?

Gary He's taken one of the make-up girls for an Indian.

Patrick I hope she likes the quiet type. I went to his place for the first time the other night. He doesn't possess one single book.

Gary No?

Patrick No. I said, 'What do you do if you want to read something? 'Read?' he says. 'Yes,' I say. 'What would you do?' 'Oh,' he says, 'if I feel like reading something I read that.' And there's a towel by his sink with George Street Municipal Baths written on it.

Gary He was joking.

Patrick He was fucking serious. And that's why women go for him. They think there has to be something going on beneath such a neanderthal exterior. Did you ever smoke weed, Gary?

Gary Once or twice.

Patrick Are you supposed to get visions?

Gary I don't think so. Why?

Patrick John gave me some. And it was like I was having an operation but they'd not given me enough anaesthetic. Someone was cutting my stomach open with a knife. Stuff like caviar was coming out of my belly. They were putting their hands in and fishing around for black pearls in my gut. What do you think that means?

Gary Is there anything you're worried about?

Patrick Is there anything I'm not worried about?

Gary 'Consider the end!'

Patrick What?

Gary It's the family motto.

Patrick Whose?

Gary Yours. The tribe of the Kennedys.

Patrick Fucking hell.

Rose and Maud enter.

Maud Hi, Dad. Gary.

Gary Here come the dancing girls.

Rose Hi, Gary. Patrick.

Maud How are you, Gary?

Gary Good.

Maud Have you heard from Judith at all?

Gary No. No, I've not.

Patrick Progeny. Who wants a drink?

Maud I'll get these.

Patrick No. You'll not deprive me of my pleasure.

Maud Two Bloody Marys then.

Patrick Gary?

Gary No. You're all right, thanks, Patrick.

Rose Tonight's the big night?

Patrick Let's not talk about it, eh? (*He goes to the bar.*)

Rose Look at Dad. He's like a schoolkid. He booked a table, you know. At the Locanda. There's never more than three people in there anyways.

Maud How are you, Gary?

Gary Good, yeah.

Maud You all ready for London?

Gary Not much to get ready, you know. Ticket. Bag.

Maud Have you seen Kevin in here tonight?

Gary He was with Gifford earlier.

Maud And the make-up girls?

Gary I don't know.

Maud He doesn't waste time, does he?

Gary I don't know who he was with, Maud. (*towards the bar*) You all right, John?

Maud Is that the Californian with him?

Rose Yeah.

Maud Do you think she can talk through those lips?

Gary I'll see yous all later.

Maud Stay, Gary. Please.

Gary I've some work I've got to finish. See you.

Rose 'Bye, Gary.

Maud 'Bye.

  Gary exits.

Rose I might go home, actually.

Maud You will not. This is our pub. He's the fucking tourist. I'll go and say hello.

Rose No. Why would you do that?

Maud See what's going on. I'll be nice to him. Make him feel awkward. Look, look . . . her tits stay still when she moves.

  Patrick comes back with the drinks. Maud goes to the bar.

Patrick Nikki's just finishing the glasses.

Rose You all right?

Patrick Why? Do I not look all right?

Rose You look great.

Patrick Not – not too dressed up?

Rose No.

Patrick You not talking to John?

Rose No.

Patrick He came and went very quickly.

Rose He did. Nikki's waving you over.

Patrick 'My master calls me. I must go.'

Patrick goes to the bar. Rose downs her drink and exits.

SCENE ELEVEN

Gary's flat. Late. Judith and Gary are sitting at his table, drinking wine together.

Judith Can I stay tonight?

Gary Should you not go home?

Judith I'm not meant to be back until Friday.

Gary Do you have no bags?

Judith I left it on the boat.

Gary Boat?

Judith I couldn't change my flight. So I got the ferry back.

Gary How was the sea?

Judith Very black.

Gary Shall I run you a bath?

Judith No. Could I possibly stay here for the week? I can't face them, Gary. Can I have a cigarette?

Gary gives her the packet. She tries to light it but can't. He lights one for her and takes hers.

Gary Stay tonight. See how you feel tomorrow.

Judith Thanks.

Gary Do you want to talk about it?

Judith You don't want me to stay till Friday?

Gary Best if you went home.

Judith You're expecting someone?

Gary Don't be ridiculous.

Judith Are you all packed for London?

Gary No. I've a few days yet.

Judith I saw her. My mum.

Gary I know. How was it?

Judith All right. Horrible.

Gary Why?

Judith She just didn't want me around, really. I got to her place the time we'd arranged and she wasn't there. So I waited in a pub across the road. She turned up an hour later. She'd had to stay late at work. We talked a bit and then I left.

Gary Where did you go?

Judith All-night caffs. She didn't ask me to stay.

Gary So what did you talk about?

Judith Not much. She put the telly on. I'd only been there about half an hour and she turned it on. I went to the toilet and burst into tears. She knew when I came back in but she didn't say anything. I told her I'd be in London a few days and she said to ring her.

Gary But you didn't?

Judith No.

Gary She was probably very nervous.

Judith Yeah. I bought her a bottle of wine. And she put it in the press. I haven't seen her in ten years and she put it away. She didn't touch me, Gary, not once.

Gary I'm sorry.

Judith Why should she touch me? Just because I wanted her to doesn't mean it was the right thing to do, does it?

Gary No.

Judith Why should she want to see me? I wasn't myself with her. My face was all fixed and my body felt stuck. My hands. I wanted her to take my hand.

Gary takes her hand.

Gary I'm sorry.

Judith She didn't look at me when we were talking. She kept looking away. I was staring at her and she kept watching the telly or the window.

Gary She probably didn't know how to handle it.

Judith Mm. She was embarrassed, Gary. My being there embarrassed her. Were you asleep?

Gary No. Are you tired?

86

Judith No. I'm still shaking with all the coffee I drunk.

Gary The bed's there when you want it. Pyjamas are here if you want them. (*indicates under the pillow*)

Judith Under the pillow?

Gary Yeah. Very rock'n'roll. I'll sleep on the floor.

Judith No, Gary, I want you next to me. But Gary, I don't . . .

Gary Shush.

Judith watches her hand, which is shaking.

Judith It won't stop. A woman there asked me for a cigarette.

Gary Where?

Judith In the caff. She was a junkie. Prostitute.

Gary Yeah?

Judith Yeah. She said she'd lost hers. And I just said I had none. And she was searching everywhere in a panic for her fags and I knew she wouldn't find them and that she'd ask me for money. She was crawling around under the table. In this tiny red dress with bruised legs. And then she found them. And she offered me one. She bought me a cup of coffee because I couldn't stop crying when she offered me a cigarette. I'd been so fucking mean in my head towards her, and I thought maybe that's why Mum doesn't really like me. Because I'm mean.

Gary You're not mean.

Judith I think I am. Cold. Yeah.

Gary You're not fucking cold and you're not mean and she's a stupid bitch for making you feel that way about yourself.

87

Judith Do you love me, Gary?

Gary I do. I'd die for you.

Judith Can we fuck?

Gary We can.

Judith Will you mind if I cry?

Gary No. No, I won't mind.

They embrace.

SCENE TWELVE

The Tiger Tandoori. Lily and John are sitting at a table drinking, having finished a huge meal. Lily is in her new blue spangly dress.

Lily Can I have another snake?

John (*to the waiter*) Another cobra, please. And a lassi.

Lily I always wanted a dog like Lassie. Do you like my dress, John? Can we play our game again?

John Absolutely. I love your dress. (*He empties some matches onto the table.*)

Lily I won last week. And the week before.

John You did, but I might win tonight. Okay . . . Yeats is walking along a river with Maud Gonne and they are looking at swans . . . I say, 'They stay together all their lives, you know.' . . . She says . . .

Lily (*thinks*) . . . 'They must get very fucking bored of each other.'

John Much better than the script. One point to you. Next line . . . Yeats meets Maud at a hotel and says, 'I felt that you came to me in a dream last night and that our souls came together in the strangest way.' She says . . .

Lily 'Shut up and kiss me.'

John Not sure about that one. It's been said before.

Lily It's what she would say. Give me a point. I want my point.

John It has to be an original line.

Lily I've never heard anyone in my life say it before. I made it up. Originally I have. I want a point.

John Either we play it properly or we don't play at all.

Lily Please. It's my point.

John If the next answer is brilliant you get all three points. Agreed? . . . Agreed?

Lily Tell me the next question before I agree.

John Unethical . . . but I concede . . . so . . . He's betrayed her by being with another woman. He says, 'Can you ever forgive me for looking at another when you were my Troy, my epiphany, my Byzantium?' Reply?

Lily 'Fuck off!'

John Three points to you. I think you should be writing the script, Lily . . . How is everyone at home? Patrick? Maud?

Lily Judith's still in London. Let's do first one to fifty.

John I don't think they stay open that late. Maud's meant to be here by now, isn't she?

Lily She'll be here. Let's play the game.

Rose enters.

Rose Lily. I'm to take you back.

Lily Why isn't Maud here? You said you never wanted to pick me up on my Indian Wednesdays.

Rose Kevin's ill.

John Would you like a drink?

Rose No.

John How are you?

Lily I've not finished my snake. Can I take it with me?

Rose I'll phone for a cab.

John Use my phone.

Rose I'll ask Nadeem. (*Rose exits to make the call.*)

Lily I think it's like heaven in here. Even the music.

John Do you want some fritters and cobras to take home with you?

Lily Yes, please, thank you very much. I'll save some for Judith too. Can I get her a snake as well? Do we have to finish the game there? I'm sorry that I'm old.

John You're as old as you feel.

Lily What if you feel nothing? You're sad?

John I'm stupid.

Lily No. You have intelligent hands.

John Do I?

Lily Do you what? Can I have some kulfi and pineapple fritters to take home? I love Wednesdays now, John.

John So do I, Lily.

Lily I'm going to ask Nadeem what fritters to have.

Lily gets up and exits as Rose comes back.

John Did you get one?

Rose Where's Lily?

John Ordering takeaways. Cigarette?

Rose Thanks.

John Why don't you sit down?

Rose sits.

Did you get my letter?

Rose Yes.

John Right . . . but you didn't reply?

Rose No. How's the film?

John Okay. It's quite intense, actually. I'm feeling much closer to Yeats than when I started.

Rose That's good, isn't it?

Lily returns.

Lily I've ordered fritters and a snake for Judith. Do you think they'll keep until she comes back? I thought of getting some for Esther in case she surprises us, but she won't, will she?

Rose No.

John Same time next week then, Lily?

Lily Yes, John.

John Good. Would you like to eat with us next week, Rose?

Rose I can't. I'm going out.

Lily With who?

Rose Nobody.

John The Secret Rose . . . Have you read those poems?

Rose No.

John The Rosicrucians believed that a rose bloomed on the cross when Christ died. That the crucifix was masculine and the rose feminine.

Lily And the cross married the rose?

John Something like that.

Rose There's the cab. 'Bye. (*Rose exits.*)

John 'Bye.

Lily Thank you, John, for being my hero tonight.

John It's a pleasure. Goodnight.

Lily Goodnight. (*Touches his face.*) Don't worry, John. About loss. Please. Promise?

John Loss?

Lily I will let you win next week.

Lily exits singing 'Goodnight My Love' to John, who sits and smokes

SCENE THIRTEEN

Rose's room. Rose is smoking a joint. Maud comes in.

Maud I'm sorry about tonight. I'm sorry. Kevin was really bad. I just couldn't leave him. Are you not talking to me?

Rose No.

Maud What are you smoking? Can I have some?

Rose passes the joint to Maud.

Could you not have asked them to put her in a cab?

Rose Like last time? When they took her to the beach because she said she lived there?

Maud I thought he might hurt himself. He was having an existential crisis.

Rose He wasn't having one. He is one. From birth to death. One long silent fucking scream.

Maud The state of the world disturbs him. I was a bastard to him, Rose. He was crying so I held him. Then he came to me naked. With the light on. And I didn't like his body. I didn't like the colour scheme. I probably would have liked it if I'd seen it from the start. But it just seemed like a foreign body . . . Did you speak to John?

Rose Sort of.

Maud What did you say?

Rose Nothing.

Maud He's fucked up, isn't he?

Rose We're all fucked up.

Maud Don't defend him.

Rose No. He has tried to apologise, though.

Maud They all apologise. They love it.

Rose What?

Maud Looking depressed and saying sorry for being so complicated. Implying we're simple or something. They should be trying to treat us in a way that doesn't warrant apology.

Rose You're right.

Maud He did not conduct himself with dignity and that's important in my book.

Rose Absolutely. Do you think I'm dignified?

Maud Very.

Rose Do you remember the day I went to the beach in a state? After I'd gone to John in the night?

Maud Yeah.

Rose You know the Kurdish guy who runs the tea van by the cliffs?

Maud Yeah.

Rose We fucked that day. On the floor of his van. It was pouring with rain and he offered me shelter. Do you think that's dignified?

Pause.

Maud . . . Yeah. I think that's great. That's poetry. You were rejected and you flew to a dark stranger by the sea. Besides that, he's gorgeous. I always went back for a Wagon Wheel separately from my tea and I don't even like chocolate. Plus he doesn't speak English, which is a huge added attraction.

Rose I don't even know his name.

Maud Last Tango in Ballina. It's perfect. Did anyone come to buy tea while you were doing it?

Rose No. He closed the shutter.

Maud Even more dignified, then.

Rose I don't know that most people would see it that way.

Maud We're not most people, thank fuck. So how did you actually lead up to it with no words?

Rose We smiled a bit. Gesticulated. Then I burst into tears. He was very beautiful. You know you said you didn't feel like you knew Mum?

94

Maud Yeah.

Rose I feel exactly the same way. But it bothers me less and less.

SCENE FOURTEEN

The kitchen. Late. Lily is by the fire. She is dressed in her new spangly blue dress and slippers. Judith walks in from outside.

Judith Hi, Lily.

Lily Hi, Lily, hi lo. You look great. Tired. You must have been partying all the time. Are they not with you? Rose and Maud went to meet you at the station.

Judith I caught an earlier train.

Lily They've been waiting ages. I've a snake for you in the fridge. And a fritter. So will you tell me everything?

Judith It was great. Mum is really well. She sends you her best.

Lily Is she working hard?

Judith She is, yeah.

Lily How was her hair?

Judith It was . . . it looked great.

Lily Long?

Judith Yeah.

Lily Good. I was worried about that. Does she have a couch and things?

Judith She does. She's got everything.

Rose and Maud come in.

Rose We were at the station. Where were you?

Judith I got in early and called in on Gary. Sorry, I didn't realise . . .

Maud How was it?

Rose How are you?

Maud How's Mum?

Judith Fine. Really good. It all went fine. She sends her best to you all. She loved your presents, Maud.

Maud Did she? What did she say?

Judith She just loved them.

Rose So what did you do? Where did you go?

Judith We stayed in and chatted most of the time. And Mum was working a lot.

Rose Did she not get time off?

Judith She couldn't, no.

Maud How is she?

Judith She's well.

Lily Did you tell her about my blue dress?

Judith I did. And she wants a photo of it.

Maud Did you take any photos?

Judith No. I forgot.

Maud I'm glad it went well. Do you feel good for seeing her?

Judith I do.

Maud I'm sorry about my being stupid. You didn't mention that to her, did you?

Judith Course I didn't. How's it all been here?

Maud Fine.

Rose Dad went on his date.

Judith My God. How did it go?

Rose They're meeting again next Tuesday.

Judith Oh my God.

Maud Tell us about Mum. From the start.

Judith Well. I got to her place and she'd cooked us a meal. And we drank wine and just talked, really.

Maud Is she going to come over soon?

Judith She's going to try, yeah.

Maud Did you go out and stuff?

Judith One night we went to a pub where they were playing music. Kilburn was great. And on the last night we went to an Italian restaurant in St John's Wood. Got completely langered.

Maud So it was brilliant?

Judith It was.

Maud I'm really happy that you had a nice time.

   Pause.

Judith I came back on Sunday. I've been at Gary's all week.

Rose What? Why?

Judith I only spent an evening with Mum and it was pretty miserable. Sorry.

Lily Get your sister a drink.

Maud gives Judith a whiskey.

Rose Why would you do that? Not come home? Why did you hide?

Judith I don't know. It seemed like the thing to do.

Rose So what was all that just now?

Judith Nothing. It just came out.

Rose We were talking about you every day. What you might be doing.

Judith I'm sorry.

Rose You hid at Gary's?

Judith You always said I was never surprising.

Rose That's not surprising, that's ridiculous.

Lily Were you scared to come home, Judith?

Judith I wasn't scared. I wasn't thinking.

Rose You were thinking pretty fast just then.

Lily Be understanding to your sister.

Rose I can't be understanding if I don't fucking understand, can I?

Judith I've been an idiot.

Rose Fucking lunatic.

Lily Don't call her a lunatic. She was frightened.

Judith I've been really stupid. I'm sorry.

Rose What were you gonna do? Keep lying to us and go and visit her again next year and camp at a fucking bus stop?

Judith No. I didn't mean to lie.

Rose So what was staying at Gary's all fucking week if it wasn't lying?

Judith I don't know. I'm sorry.

Rose Fuck sorry.

Judith What do you want me to say, Rose? What do you want me to do? You tell me and I'll do it, all right? Okay?

Rose No. It's not fucking okay!

Judith So what the fuck do you want me to do?

Maud Stop it, Rose! Judith, please!

Lily Don't shout, don't shout. I want to see Esther! Where is she?

Rose She's in London where she fucking belongs!

Maud Don't, Rose, please please.

Lily I want to see her. I want to see Esther! Are you teasing me? Have you hidden her somewhere? Esther! Esther!

Judith She's not here, Lily. She's not coming here.

Lily She will! Don't you tell me what she will or won't do. Don't you tell me I'm a child or I'm a lunatic.

Maud Lily, it's all right.

Lily Everyone leaves. They've all gone. They've all gone. (*Lily puts her hands over her ears and shouts and cries.*) 'My heart is like wax . . . my heart is like wax' . . . 'I cry in the daytime but thou hearest me not; and in the night season, am not silent. I cry in the daytime but thou hearest me not and in the night season am not silent.' Make love with me, you fuckers. Make love with me! Make love with me!

Maud Lily, it's all right. We're not fighting. It's all right.

Lily I cry . . . I cry . . . I do . . . I cry . . . (*becoming more and more upset*) Make love with me! Make love with me . . . make love . . . make love with me . . . someone . . . please . . . please . . . make love with me, you fuckers! You fuckers! You fuckers!

Judith It's all right, Lily. We'll make love with you, won't we?

Rose We will, Lily . . . we will . . .

Rose holds Lily. Lily becomes abstracted and starts to look for Esther around the room.

Lily I want to see Esther! Where is she? Where's Esther? I don't want to go away! Is she hiding? Did she come back with you? Don't tease me. Please.

Judith Lily . . . she's not here . . .

Lily No. No, I see that. Yes.

Rose She never was fucking here.

Lily Don't you dare say that! Who are you anyway? Who are you? Who the fuck are you? Who are you all? Shouting and screaming . . . I'm not fucking dead, I'm not, I'm not . . .

She collapses into tears. The girls go to her and they hold each other.

I want my music. I want to hear Esther. Can I play it, please?

Rose Play what, Lily? What shall we put on?

Lily Esther. She's with her. With Kitty. Over there.

Judith No. She's alive, Lily. She's in London.

Lily She's here with Kitty. I'll play her to you.

Lily gets up and goes to Kitty's urn. From it she takes an old tape, wipes the ashes off and puts it on. She sits down with the girls. The voice is pure with a guitar. . Esther sings a few lines of Ivory Joe Hunter's 'Since I Met You Baby'.

Esther's Voice Did that sound right? Was it on? Is it on?

Patrick's Voice It's on, it's turning, look.

Esther's Voice But there's no microphone?

Patrick's Voice No, it's inside. It's that bit there. Go on.

Esther's Voice Shall I rewind it?

Patrick's Voice No, just carry on there. No one's going to hear it, are they?

Esther sings a few more bars of the song and hums to it. The girls and Lily listen.

SCENE FIFTEEN

The library. Morning. Judith is sorting through returned books. Gary enters and puts one on her pile.

Judith (*not looking up*) Thanks.

Gary Judith.

Judith Gary.

Gary Listen, I can't meet you later. I'm getting an earlier flight.

Judith I can't get cover here until two.

Gary No matter. That's why I came. To say goodbye now.

Judith Why have you changed your flight?

Gary Something came up.

Judith Who?

Gary Not someone. Something.

Judith Oh. Is this it, then?

Gary It's nice to say goodbye in here anyway. Seems appropriate. My last visit to the temple.

Judith Will you write?

Gary No.

Judith Phone me, then.

Gary You've no phone.

Judith Here. At lunchtimes.

Gary I'll see how it goes.

Judith Thank you, Gary. For last week. Everything.

Gary I'll see you.

Judith You take care.

Gary kisses her on the cheek.

Gary Say goodbye to your family for me.

Judith Will you come back for Christmas?

Gary I doubt it. (*He walks away.*)

Judith (*shouting after him*) Gary!

Gary What?

Judith I'm pregnant.

Gary You're pregnant?

Judith No. I'm not. I just always wanted to say it in here.

Gary Right. Odd.

Judith Me?

Gary Yes. You. Anything else you'd like to shock the world with, or can I go now?

Judith You can go now.

Gary Okay. (*He starts to leave.*)

Judith Gary!

Gary Yes.

Judith I wish I was pregnant.

Gary Do you?

Judith Yes. I wish I was going to have your child.

Gary Right.

   Pause.

Judith What are you thinking?

Gary I was thinking about Miss Cooper. Our old English teacher. When they locked her in the cupboard . . . Just came into my mind.

Judith Anything else?

Gary No.

Judith Right.

Gary Can you renew these books for me, Judith?

Judith I thought you didn't believe in renewals.

Gary Today's an exception.

Judith What time's your flight?

Gary No time.

Judith Good . . . Will you meet me after work?

Gary I will.

Judith I'll buy you tea.

Gary Yes. You will. I'll wait for you. Next to the graffiti.
(*He leaves*.)

SCENE SIXTEEN

*The kitchen. Evening. Rose and John are sitting drinking,
dressed in black.*

Rose Is the film finished?

John They're editing it now.

Rose Will it be good?

John No. How are you?

Rose All right. I just miss her. Already. I find this the
hardest room to be in.

John Maybe you should go away for a while.

Rose I hope she wasn't lonely when she died. Or scared.

John She was very tough.

Rose No. She wasn't. She wasn't tough at all. You were
her last love. She used to come back from the Indian like
a schoolgirl.

John Why don't you come to London for a break?

Rose What would I do in London?

John Rest. Go to the park. See the pelicans.

Rose Pelicans?

John In St James's Park.

Rose I've never seen a pelican.

Patrick, Maud, Judith and Gary enter. Judith carries
the funeral urn of Lily's ashes and places it on the table.

Patrick (*lighting a cigarette*) It was good of you to come over, John.

Judith She'd have been really happy to know you were here.

Gary She would. When you going back, John?

John Tomorrow.

Patrick Fucking stupid speech that priest made.

Maud It was what Lily asked for.

Patrick Doesn't make it any better, does it? The last request of a lunatic doesn't make it any more acceptable, does it?

Maud The music was nice.

Patrick They played it too quiet. Where's a fucking ashtray? Why do people come into other people's houses and tidy things away when someone dies? Why do they do that?

Judith I don't know. I didn't know who that woman was who was sweeping under the sofa. But I didn't like to ask. She was crying so hard.

Patrick With the one eye and a built-up shoe?

Judith Yeah.

Patrick That was Maureen. Lily and her were at school together. Fantastic dancer she is.

Maud I told Mum we'd ring her. Tell her how it went.

Patrick The world and his fucking wife turned up, didn't they? Nobody comes to see her while she's around but they get their best fucking dress on for a party. Who wants a drink?

Maud I'll do it, Dad.

Gary Is Nikki not coming round?

Maud She's getting the pub ready.

Patrick Yeah. She's done a nice spread. Sandwiches. Cake. If ever I go to hospital to die, don't let me lie there with all the tubes, will you? Pull them down. Burst the blood bags. Shoot me, but don't just leave me there without my tobacco. Will you?

Maud No, Dad.

Patrick And no fucking speeches. I've had enough of fucking words. I don't mind what hell is like as long as nobody tries to fucking talk to me.

Maud starts pouring drinks and gives one to Patrick. Judith takes one to Gary and sits on his knee. Patrick downs his drink. Maud refills his glass.

Gary (*raises his glass*) Lily O'Hanlon.

They raise their glasses to her.

Judith Did you talk to Kevin?

Maud Just said hello. He's going to Russia. Moscow. To visit Bakunin's grave.

Patrick He's always going to fucking Russia. He's been saying he's going to Russia for the past five fucking years. (*He raises his glass.*)

The weight of this sad time we must obey;
Speak what we feel, not what we ought to say.

He takes the lid off the funeral urn and uses it as an ashtray. Everyone watches.

What? Lily wouldn't have minded. She was a madwoman. Ashes to ashes.

He cries. Maud goes to him.

Maud Dad . . . Dad.

Patrick Put some fucking music on, hey?

Judith puts on a record. Marlene Dietrich singing 'Falling in Love Again' . . . They listen.

Maud Do you want to dance, Dad?

They get up and dance. The others watch. Judith and Gary dance too.

John Will you dance, Rose?

Rose No. Thanks.

Patrick Will you get off your ass, you miserable fucking spinster?

Rose dances with John. Coloured lights cascade and make the room into one of Lily's dream dance halls.

Blackout.